COMMITTED TO SIKHISM

A SIKH COMMUNITY

SYLVIA AND BARRY SUTCLIFFE

RELIGIOUS AND MORAL EDUCATION PRESS

Religious and Moral Education Press
An imprint of Chansitor Publications Ltd,
a wholly owned subsidiary of Hymns Ancient & Modern Ltd
St Mary's Works, St Mary's Plain
Norwich, Norfolk NR3 3BH

Copyright © 1995 Sylvia and Barry Sutcliffe

Sylvia and Barry Sutcliffe have asserted their right under the Copyright, Designs and Patents Act, 1988, to be identified as Authors of this Work.

All rights reserved. No part of this publication may be reproduced, stored in a retrieval system, or transmitted, in any form or by any means, electronic, electrostatic, magnetic tape, mechanical, photocopying, recording or otherwise, without permission in writing from the publishers.

First published 1995

ISBN 1-85175-027-4

Acknowledgements

The Authors and Publisher would like to thank the Sri Guru Singh Sabha, Hounslow, Middlesex, and particularly Mr Ranjit Singh, its President, for help and encouragement during all stages of the preparation of this book. We are also indebted to the interviewees for sharing with us their experiences and giving this project their time and support.

We are also grateful to Daler Singh for his assistance with photography and to Articles of Faith, Bury, Lancashire, and Exsports, Exeter, for the loan of several items used in photography.

Designed and typeset by Topics Visual Information, Exeter

Photography by Michael Burton-Pye

Printed in Singapore by Tien Wah Press for
Chansitor Publications Ltd, Norwich

CONTENTS

INTRODUCTION	4
ABOUT ME	5
WHERE I BELONG	16
WHAT I FEEL STRONGLY ABOUT	19
MY FAVOURITE FESTIVAL	24
A SPECIAL MOMENT	32
WORDS THAT MEAN A LOT TO ME	38
THINGS I FIND CHALLENGING	44
INDEX	48

INTRODUCTION

The books in this **Faith and Commitment** series give you the chance to look at religions and religious denominations (groups within religions) through the personal reflections of people with a religious commitment.

To create these books, we visited local religious communities in different parts of Britain. We talked to people across the range of ages and roles you'd expect to find in a community – parent, child, grandparent, priest, community worker. That is, we interviewed people like you and your family, your friends, the people where you live. We asked them all the same questions and we've used the themes of those questions as chapter headings in the books.

Each chapter contains extracts from those interviews. People interpret our questions as they want to. They talk freely in their own words about religious ideas and personal experiences, putting emphasis where they think it belongs for them. The result is a set of very individual insights into what religion means to some of the people who practise it. A lot of the insights are spiritual ones, so you may have had similar thoughts and experiences yourself, whether or not you consider yourself a 'religious' person.

You will see that some pages include FACT-FINDER boxes. These are linked to what people say in the interview extracts on these pages. They give you bits of back-up information, such as a definition or where to look up a reference to a prayer or a piece of scripture. Remember that these books are not textbooks. We expect you to do some research of your own when you need to. There are plenty of sources to go to and your teacher will be able to help.

There are also photographs all through the books. Some of the items you can see belong to the people whose interview extracts appear on those pages. Most of these items have personal significance. Some have religious or cultural significance, too. They are very special to the people who lent them for particular but different reasons, like special things belonging to you.

Committed to Sikhism: A Sikh Community introduces you to eight Sikhs who go to the Sri Guru Singh Sabha gurdwara in Hounslow, Middlesex. 'Sri' is a word of respect, 'sabha' is an organization. Sabhas are formed and managed by local Sikh communities to give practical support to the Sikh way of life. The biggest task of a sabha is setting up and running a gurdwara.

SYLVIA AND BARRY SUTCLIFFE

ABOUT ME

ABOUT ME

NAME: *Manjit Kaur B*

WHAT I DO: *I'm fourteen. I live in Buckinghamshire and go to school in Chalfont St Peter. We live in quite a posh area. At school, I'm in my first GCSE year, doing French, English, Maths, Science, Business Studies, Statistics and History. Eventually, I want to do something in management or business.*

SOME OF MY SPECIAL INTERESTS: *When I haven't got homework, I'll read. Novels mainly, things like Jilly Cooper.*

MY ROLE IN THE RELIGIOUS COMMUNITY

We come to this gurdwara from time to time, but more often we go to Slough because that's closer to home.

Every Sunday I go to Punjabi school. I've been going to Punjabi school since I was seven, first in Southall, now in Slough. I'm doing a GCSE in Punjabi.

I'm learning kirtan. That's a form of hymn singing accompanied by the harmonium, which I play. Someone comes to our house to teach us. So I spend part of my time practising kirtan. On Sundays, sometimes we perform in temples. Four of us from my family do that.

FACT-FINDER

Punjabi
Language spoken by people from the Punjab, a region in north-west India and south-east Pakistan where the Sikh religion began. Also the language of most of the Guru Granth Sahib, the Sikhs' sacred scriptures.

Kirtan
The hymns sung in kirtan are sacred songs from the Guru Granth Sahib (see above).

ABOUT ME

NAME: Pritpal Singh B

WHAT I DO: I go to school at Chalfont Community College, where I'm studying for A-levels in French, Geography and English. I hope to go on to university and do something computer related or in business management. Possibly even teaching. I'm keeping my options open at the moment.

I've also got a part-time job. The company I work for is putting me on an Effective Management Skills training course which should get me promotion. It'll also be helpful in getting me into university.

SOME OF MY SPECIAL INTERESTS: I don't have a lot of time for hobbies, with three A-levels and a part-time job. Religion actually is a hobby of mine as well as being a part of my life.

MY ROLE IN THE RELIGIOUS COMMUNITY

In the temple, we don't actually have fixed roles. Everyone takes part in the services every evening and on Sunday, so there's no particular role that anyone specifically has. As long as they know what they're doing, anyone can take part. For example, anyone's welcome to read from the Guru Granth Sahib as long as they know how and have had the lessons which you require to be able to read it.

I'm learning how to read the Guru Granth Sahib at the moment. I've got about a quarter of it, the last quarter, left to learn. I don't read it myself at the temple. I have read the Guru Granth Sahib in public once, but only briefly. You're supposed to complete your learning before you do.

FACT-FINDER

Guru Granth Sahib
The Sikhs' sacred scriptures. Its language is mainly Punjabi (see opposite). The script it is written in is called Gurmukhi.

ABOUT ME

NAME: Tejpreet Pal Singh

WHAT I DO: I'm fifteen. I go to Lampton School, which is the local school.

MY FAMILY: I've got one brother and one sister.

MY ROLE IN THE RELIGIOUS COMMUNITY: I come to the gurdwara every Sunday. I do a bit of sewa, going to the shoe-room and helping out there. I take in the shoes of worshippers as they come in and give out the numbers. Sometimes, upstairs in the gurdwara itself, I do kirtan.

SOME OF MY SPECIAL INTERESTS: I like playing football, cricket, general sport and basketball.

FACT-FINDER

Sewa
Performing sewa, voluntary service for others, within and outside the Sikh community, is one of the duties of all Sikhs. Running a gurdwara is a big undertaking. Most of the work of keeping gurdwaras going is done by volunteers.

Shoe-room
Worshippers and visitors to a gurdwara must take off their shoes when they arrive. At the Sri Guru Singh Sabha in Hounslow, volunteers like Tejpreet and Bachittar (see opposite) often have hundreds of pairs of shoes to look after until their owners are ready to leave.

Kirtan
Singing hymns (sacred songs) from the Guru Granth Sahib, the Sikhs' sacred scriptures.

ABOUT ME

NAME: *Bachittar Singh*

WHAT I DO: *I go to Lampton School, where I'm in Year 10. Next year I'll be taking my GCSEs. I want to get educated, get a good job – preferably in law. I'd like to be a solicitor.*

MY FAMILY: *I've got three sisters.*

MY ROLE IN THE RELIGIOUS COMMUNITY: *I attend the gurdwara quite frequently – every Sunday and maybe twice in the week if I can. Sometimes I'll help out collecting the shoes or working in the langar, where I'll clear plates or possibly serve food. Usually, I go upstairs into the prayer hall and listen to the kirtan.*

SOME OF MY SPECIAL INTERESTS: *I enjoy playing football but like any sport, really – karate, tennis. I'm into anything. I play cricket and football for the school.*

FACT-FINDER

Collecting the shoes
Worshippers and visitors to a gurdwara must take off their shoes when they arrive. (See opposite.)

Langar
Every gurdwara has a langar, a kitchen/dining hall where members of the Sikh community and any visitors can always share a free meal. The term 'langar' is also used for the meal itself. The food for the langar is provided by the Sikh community, who also share the cooking, washing-up, etc. (See also page 13.)

Kirtan
Singing hymns (sacred songs) from the Guru Granth Sahib, the Sikhs' sacred scriptures.

ABOUT ME

NAME: *Raminder Singh V*

WHAT I DO: *I'm thirty-five. I came to this country from East Africa when I was nine. Most of my education has been here – secondary school in Birmingham, A-levels. After school, I worked for the Inland Revenue then for British Airways before going to university and training to be a teacher. I started teaching in 1985. Now I'm Headteacher of a middle school in Berkshire.*

MY FAMILY: *I'm one of four children. My father died in 1984 and my older brother and sister live in America, so I'm more or less head of the family here. I'm married with two children of my own. Tejpal, my son, is four-and-a-half years old. Rupi, my daughter, is just eighteen months.*

SOME OF MY SPECIAL INTERESTS: *I'm a keen sportsman – I play cricket and hockey at Ashford Sports Club. I also love to travel. Aneet and I normally have two holidays abroad a year.*

MY ROLE IN THE RELIGIOUS COMMUNITY

As far as the community is concerned, I help during the summer holidays with the gurdwara summer school. I'm very interested in developing Sikh culture and identity. I feel that the way society generally and the education system in particular is going, the cultural identity of communities like this one in Hounslow will gradually disappear unless people take determined action. So the role of the gurdwara and of community leaders, not just Sikh community leaders, is vital.

Being a headteacher, I have a relatively high community profile. My role is using that wherever I can. For instance, I'm a member of the Hounslow SACRE, a group that advises Hounslow Education Authority about its RE syllabus for schools.

FACT-FINDER

SACRE
The Standing Advisory Council for Religious Education which, by law, must be set up by each education authority.

ABOUT ME

NAME: Aneet Kaur V

WHAT I DO: I'm thirty-three years old and married with two children. I call myself a mother rather than a housewife. I feel it's important that I'm at home to look after my children, so I'm not working at the moment. I used to work in a bank.

MY ROLE IN THE RELIGIOUS COMMUNITY: I don't take part in the community as much as I'd like to because I don't have the time. I do get a lot of parents at the school where my husband used to be Deputy Head, and who know me, coming up and saying, 'Our child is moving away from the culture. There's a lot of peer pressure. What can we do?' or 'We've got a problem. What can we do?' I find I'm often talking to children or their parents. In a lot of cases, parents can be too rigid in their views.

SOME OF MY SPECIAL INTERESTS: I like swimming and reading. I also help out in the local school in my free time, but with two very young children I don't have much of that!

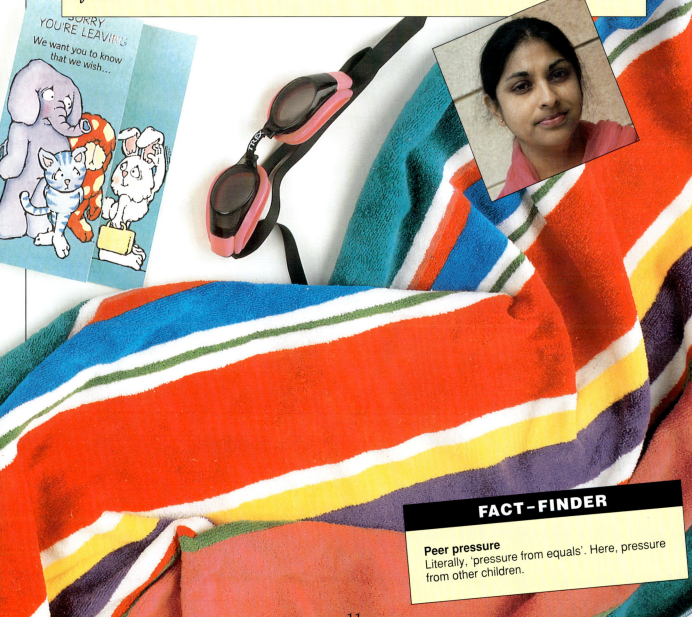

FACT-FINDER

Peer pressure
Literally, 'pressure from equals'. Here, pressure from other children.

ABOUT ME

NAME: Ranjit Singh

Singh isn't a family name or a surname as some people think. It's a way of naming a Sikh. Ranjit is my personal name, so with the Sikh name added I'm Ranjit Singh. I never use my family name with it. That's my choice.

WHAT I DO: I'm a school teacher, retired now. I worked with a neighbouring education authority for about eleven years, then I was Co-ordinator for Community Languages in the London Borough of Ealing for eleven or twelve years. I'm more or less committed to the Sabha, to the community, now.

MY FAMILY: My wife works in central London as a civil servant with the Department of Trade and Industry. She's a very religious lady, a committed Sikh. I've got one son and one daughter, both married. My son is a researcher/speechwriter for several MPs in the House of Commons. He's the only turbanned boy there! My daughter has an honours degree in computing and is married to a doctor. My son lives with us. My daughter lives with her husband in Richmond.

ABOUT ME

FACT-FINDER

Singh
Literally, 'lion'. This name was first given to male Sikhs by Guru Gobind Singh at the first Baisakhi, when the Khalsa, the organization or fellowship of pure Sikhs, was started (see pages 26–27). Female members of the Khalsa take the name Kaur, meaning 'princess'.

MY ROLE IN THE RELIGIOUS COMMUNITY

I've been working in the Sikh community for a long time. In Southall there's a big Sikh temple, the biggest in England, with about 15 000 members. I was General Secretary there, and Treasurer for a while. Then, in 1978, people here in Hounslow realized they needed their own gurdwara. So we started our own organization, the Sri Guru Singh Sabha, of which I'm currently President.

To start with, we held meetings once a month in Hounslow in a rented school hall. Three years later, we bought a plot of land for about £60 000. Since then, we've spent nearly £3 million developing a purpose-built gurdwara. We raised the money ourselves. No grants. Every penny came from the Sikh community. I think it must be the best gurdwara building in England. We had over 20 000 people at the opening, some from as far away as Glasgow and Edinburgh. All the traffic was jammed in Hounslow!

Running the gurdwara is a big undertaking. We get about a thousand people using the gurdwara every week, as well as visitors. The most important thing in the gurdwara is the free community kitchen. From morning until evening, everyone is welcome to come to the kitchen and have a cup of tea or something to eat. That's every day of the week. Whoever comes is welcomed.

ABOUT ME

NAME: Partap Singh

WHAT I DO: I'm seventy-one years old, born into a Sikh family. My family moved from India to Kenya when I was born. I went back to India with my mother (my father stayed behind in Kenya) and I was brought up and educated there. Later I returned to Kenya as a qualified mechanical and electrical engineer and worked for almost thirty years in the administration and management of a large textile mill. By the mid-Seventies it was Kenyan Government policy for local people to do the jobs of expatriates like me wherever possible. This policy was called Africanization, and in 1975 I lost my job because of it.

That was the year I came to Britain. I had a house in Britain and my children were already studying here. I started all over again with whatever job I could get. Now I'm working in London as an accountant. Still working, that is.

MY ROLE IN THE RELIGIOUS COMMUNITY: I was elected President of a Sikh temple in Thika, an industrial town in Kenya, and remained its President and Chairman for about fifteen years. Thika is twenty miles from Nairobi, and there used to be a lot of Sikhs and Gujaratis there – working in the textile mill and in the coffee, sisal and pine-apple plantations. During this period I did a lot of community welfare work, not only with Sikhs but with other people living locally. 'Service' is my motto. It's something I enjoy giving.

SOME OF MY SPECIAL INTERESTS: I like reading religious books and literature and learning about other religions. My favourite games are tennis, golf and snooker, and I've been quite good at them in my time! I also do community work with people in need.

ABOUT ME

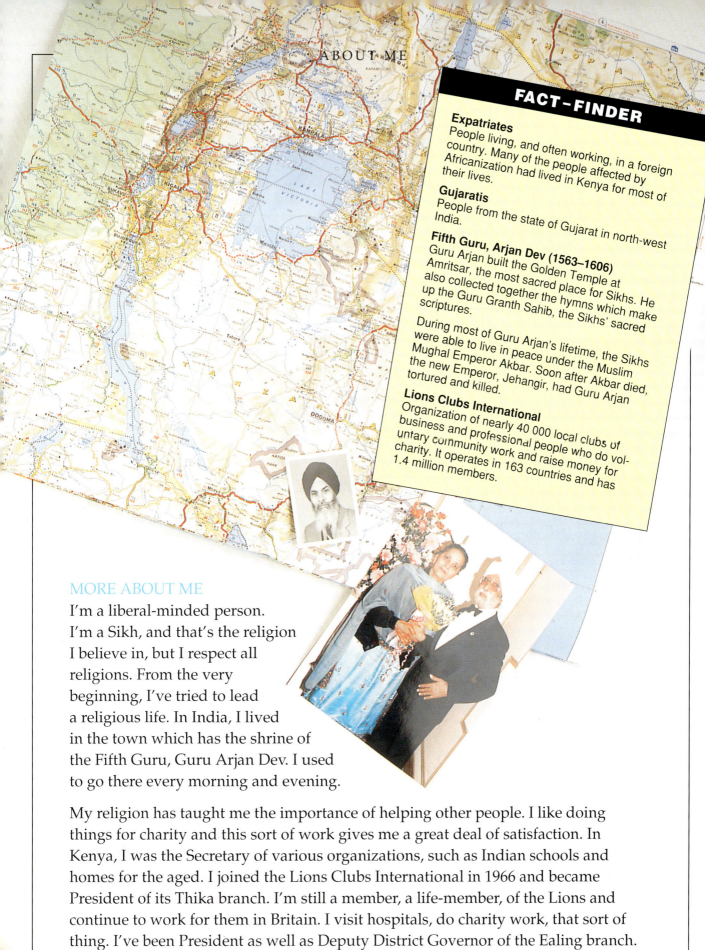

FACT-FINDER

Expatriates
People living, and often working, in a foreign country. Many of the people affected by Africanization had lived in Kenya for most of their lives.

Gujaratis
People from the state of Gujarat in north-west India.

Fifth Guru, Arjan Dev (1563–1606)
Guru Arjan built the Golden Temple at Amritsar, the most sacred place for Sikhs. He also collected together the hymns which make up the Guru Granth Sahib, the Sikhs' sacred scriptures.

During most of Guru Arjan's lifetime, the Sikhs were able to live in peace under the Muslim Mughal Emperor Akbar. Soon after Akbar died, the new Emperor, Jehangir, had Guru Arjan tortured and killed.

Lions Clubs International
Organization of nearly 40 000 local clubs of business and professional people who do voluntary community work and raise money for charity. It operates in 163 countries and has 1.4 million members.

MORE ABOUT ME

I'm a liberal-minded person. I'm a Sikh, and that's the religion I believe in, but I respect all religions. From the very beginning, I've tried to lead a religious life. In India, I lived in the town which has the shrine of the Fifth Guru, Guru Arjan Dev. I used to go there every morning and evening.

My religion has taught me the importance of helping other people. I like doing things for charity and this sort of work gives me a great deal of satisfaction. In Kenya, I was the Secretary of various organizations, such as Indian schools and homes for the aged. I joined the Lions Clubs International in 1966 and became President of its Thika branch. I'm still a member, a life-member, of the Lions and continue to work for them in Britain. I visit hospitals, do charity work, that sort of thing. I've been President as well as Deputy District Governor of the Ealing branch.

WHERE I BELONG

I've lived in England for twenty-nine years. I trained as a teacher here. I've taught here. Nevertheless, I feel that I belong to the Punjab. Guru Gobind Singh, the Tenth Master, baptized the Sikhs at Anandpur, a place in the Punjab. Guru Nanak, founder of the Sikh religion, was born in the Punjab. I lived in the Punjab for the first thirty-five years of my life and my parents, my brother and sister and their families are still there – that's in the Indian part of the Punjab. When India was divided in 1947, the Punjab was split. Guru Nanak's birthplace is now in Pakistan, for example.

I went to India last year, after my retirement. I used to be a teacher in the Punjab, and a head-teacher. I founded a school there. When I visited it, the memories came flooding back. Wherever I went, people kept asking me when I was going to return.

But the ties are getting looser. My children are not anxious to go back, and I'm too old. I've kept my Indian nationality, just in case. But my family's here and I can't be divided from them. I know I will stay here until the end of life.

RANJIT SINGH

> **FACT-FINDER**
>
> **Punjab**
> The Punjab, the region of north-west India where the Sikh religion began, was split when (in 1947) India became independent of British rule. The part of the Punjab which is now within (Muslim) Pakistan is more than twice the size of the modern Indian state of Punjab.
>
> **Guru Gobind Singh ...**
> Ranjit is talking about the first Baisakhi (see pages 26–27), when Guru Gobind Singh, the Tenth Guru, founded the Khalsa, the organization or fellowship of pure Sikhs.

I suppose, although I was born in Britain, I feel that I partly belong to India. That's where my ancestors come from. The whole Sikh tradition's from there. I would be prepared to go and live in India and adopt that as my home, and I think my sisters would say the same.

When my parents talk about home, they mean India and the Punjab. That's where they're from. But when I talk about home, I mean Britain. It is my home at the moment.

BACHITTAR SINGH

WHERE I BELONG

I belong in Britain, although my roots are firmly based in India. My cultural identity is Indian and not English, so I don't pass the Norman Tebbit 'cricket test'. During test matches between India and England, I will always support India.

I belong to the Sikh community. My parents and also the educational system in the U.K. have given me a lot. Now I feel it's time to put something back in. My parents were a strong influence on my attitudes and I believe strongly in the things they valued – especially community life and the value of the extended family. Now it's time for me to give.

I don't want the next generation to go through the same hardships that I had to deal with. It's my responsibility to help them, and my role as a headteacher is an influential one. I want the children in my care to be able to grow up confidently as individuals, respecting what makes others individual. That's what my school policies aim towards. Helping children grow up as confident individuals is what I feel I belong doing.

RAMINDER SINGH V

FACT-FINDER

Norman Tebbit 'cricket test'
In April 1990, British politician Norman Tebbit caused controversy by criticizing British Asians who failed his 'cricket test', i.e. cheered the Indian cricket side rather than England.

Extended family
Parents and children living as one large family with grandparents, aunts, uncles and/or cousins, etc., often sharing the same house.

When I go to Punjabi school, I feel better there because I can relate to the others better. We share a lot of the same interests, do most things the same. I don't have to explain myself.

At English school there are no Indian students. Sometimes I can bring up a topic and find I'm having to explain what I'm talking about.

I don't see myself as English, but I don't see myself as Indian, either. When someone says 'Indian', I think of a person who's come from India, and I haven't. I just consider myself a Sikh.

MANJIT KAUR B

FACT-FINDER

Punjabi school
Classes on Sundays at the gurdwara where Manjit learns the Punjabi language (see page 6) and about her religion.

English school
Manjit means the 'ordinary' school she attends on weekdays.

WHERE I BELONG

I am a British Sikh. I belong in Britain. I've lived here all my life. The only difference between me and the majority of other people is a religious one.

This is going to sound a bit political, but I see it like this. I don't think anyone can say they're purely British. What does that mean? Throughout history, there have been invasions of these islands – by Romans, Vikings, Normans, all sorts of people. They've brought different languages and different cultures with them. All I can say is that I'm just another invader. Well, not me. My parents, anyway.

PRITPAL SINGH B

I originally came from Africa, but I've spent most of my childhood in this country and grown up here. I've only been to India a couple of times. So I think I belong in Britain. But what I am is a Sikh. It's very important to me that I carry that identity. It doesn't matter where I am, I'm still a Sikh.

ANEET KAUR V

I belong to a middle-class, devoted Sikh family which works hard to demonstrate faithful living, truthful living and honesty. I try hard to live by these principles and pass them on to my children and grandchildren. I also try to help other people if I can, people who are less fortunate than myself.

PARTAP SINGH

I belong in the Sikh community, but if you're asking about my country of origin, I come from India. I was actually born in the Middle East, in Oman, and lived there for about eight years. Then we went to India but left because of the troubles. So, at the moment, Britain is where my home is. In the future, though, I'd like to go back to the Middle East. I don't know about my family, but that's something I'd like to do.

TEJPREET PAL SINGH

FACT-FINDER

Troubles in India
Tejpreet is talking about the early 1980s, when there was increasing conflict in the Punjab between Sikhs and the Indian Government. The situation exploded in 1984, when Indian troops stormed the Golden Temple at Amritsar.

WHAT I FEEL STRONGLY ABOUT

I believe strongly in valuing individuality. In the 70s and early 80s, integration was the theory of the day. I don't believe at all in integration. What's more important to me is valuing the things, like culture, that make people individual. We have to have an outlook and opinions which we're not afraid of expressing.

I went through a phase in my life when I did a lot of compromising. I had to compromise just to be accepted. You want to be accepted by everyone so you try to be like them. I did that for a long time. I started losing my values – but I'm not sure what I really got in return. I think I was taken advantage of in some ways. Even now, Sikh children at school are under similar sorts of pressure. They cut their hair because they get teased about it.

I do a fair amount of work in RE with teachers in other schools and trainee teachers. I don't think the new legislation about RE and collective worship in schools is particularly encouraging. How can I possibly go into a school and expect an assembly of mainly Hindus, Muslims and Sikhs to take part in an act of worship which values Christianity more than their faiths? I can't do that.

This Sikh community has been particularly good about making sure there are plenty of learning resources about Sikh religion and culture available to our children. It gives a lot of money to local schools to develop materials about Sikhism. As a headteacher, I'm keen to support initiatives that recognize cultural diversity as a positive aspect of people's identity.

RAMINDER SINGH V

FACT-FINDER

Integration
Here, the idea that immigrants should be encouraged to adapt themselves to the 'British way of life' not just to overcome practical difficulties, but with the aim of becoming, eventually, as much like 'everyone else' as possible.

New legislation ...
The Education Reform Act 1988 and follow-up laws made in the early 1990s said that pupils should spend something like half their time in RE studying Christianity and that each school must hold daily acts of collective worship 'mainly of a broadly Christian nature'.

WHAT I FEEL STRONGLY ABOUT

I feel very strongly about religion. It plays a very important part in my life. Sikhism is, I believe, a way of life. It's not something you have one day but not the next. It's an 'every minute' thing. I'm very proud of my identity. Hence the turban – and the beard, which I'm trying to grow!

Sikhism is a commitment. For instance, if you're a Sikh, every morning you have to say five allocated prayers. You also have to say an evening prayer and a bedtime prayer. This is a part of your life. You have to fit it in. It doesn't mean that I don't go out with my friends, enjoy myself. But if someone says, 'Go on, try this!' and it's alcohol, perhaps, or something else which is prohibited, I'll put my foot down and say no, full stop.

I don't resent any part of my religion and what it requires me to do. If I did, I wouldn't be sitting here now. I'm very proud of it. People respect me as well, which is the nice thing. Where I live in Buckinghamshire I'm the only Sikh, apart from my family. None of my friends are Sikhs. But my friends respect my beliefs and my religion. In fact, they're very interested in it. They often ask 'How do you do this?' or 'What do you think about that?' So I'm a bit of a religious adviser myself.

PRITPAL SINGH B

FACT-FINDER

Turban ... beard
Uncut hair (including an uncut beard) is one of the Five K's, the five symbols worn by Sikhs who are members of the Khalsa, the organization or fellowship of pure Sikhs. Usually Sikh men wear a turban, not just to keep their hair tidy, but also so that everyone can see that they are Sikhs.

WHAT I FEEL STRONGLY ABOUT

I care about my religion. At the moment, I've just become a Khalsa Sikh – I've had the Amrit ceremony. I was initiated at Baisakhi this year. What I'm really interested in is keeping pure, not eating meat any more, not drinking alcohol, not smoking, things like that. I'd say I care about my religion a lot.

> **FACT-FINDER**
>
> **Khalsa • Amrit • Baisakhi**
> Sikhs are initiated into (become members of) the Khalsa, the organization or fellowship of pure Sikhs, at a ceremony using Amrit (sacred sugared water). Baisakhi is an annual festival celebrating the founding of the Khalsa by Guru Gobind Singh. (See also pages 26–27.)
>
> **Cut their hair**
> Uncut hair is one of the Five K's, the five symbols worn by Sikhs.

There's a lot of pressure now I'm an initiated Sikh. First of all, in the family, because I'm the only one who's had Amrit. The rest of my family hasn't. If they have meat, I'm not allowed to eat it, so I'm the one left out. And I did used to like the old sausage and stuff! But our Gurus committed their lives, and some of them lost their lives, for our religion. The least I can do is give up eating meat.

Then there are my friends. They do drink, they do smoke. Occasionally they ask me to come along with them and I'm standing there, the odd one out. Then I do feel, 'Why can't I do this?' But they respect what I've done. It was my choice to become a Khalsa Sikh. I have to admit that when I was thinking about it, I wondered whether they'd take the mickey out of me. But they respect me. I realize they respect me now. Some of my Sikh friends, they cut their hair but they do go to the gurdwara. Maybe one day some of them will be initiated, too.

TEJPREET PAL SINGH

I feel strongly about my family and my religion. Our family's very big. Mum and Dad, my brothers and sisters and my dad's five brothers and their families all live together. That's why we've got a big house. We all respond to each other as we're brothers and sisters or cousins. We've been together all our lives.

We and four of Dad's brothers and their families live in the big house. The fifth brother's family lives in the bungalow. It's quite fun! We have our moments.

I'm very intense about my religion. I feel it very strongly. I like finding out things about it. You can find out more about the Sikh religion when you come here to the temple, and at Punjabi school to some extent, although that's also about learning the Punjabi language. Sometimes the school runs workshops where you can find out about Sikh history – like they did in the summer holidays. I enjoyed that.

MANJIT KAUR B

FACT-FINDER

Punjabi school
Classes on Sundays at the gurdwara where Manjit learns the Punjabi language (see page 6) and about her religion.

WHAT I FEEL STRONGLY ABOUT

I feel very strongly about my identity. I am a Sikh, and what is very, very important to me is bringing up my children as Sikhs, helping them learn the true values of Sikhism. Hopefully, when they grow up, they'll be able to reflect back over what we, as parents, have taught them and realize that, wherever they happen to be living, they belong to the Sikh faith.

Last week we were in the Southgate gurdwara celebrating Baisakhi. I always find the ceremony of the flag-changing, which we do every year, very emotional. At that time perhaps more than any other the community stands together as one. You feel that you belong to the community. When it was over, I asked Tejpal, our four-and-a-half year old, 'Are you proud to be Sikh?' He turned to me and said, 'Yes, Mummy, I *am* proud to be Sikh.' I thought that was wonderful.

ANEET KAUR V

FACT-FINDER

Values
Ideas about what is right, what is wrong, what is of real value in life and how people should behave.

Baisakhi
Festival celebrating the founding of the Khalsa, the organization or fellowship of pure Sikhs, by Guru Gobind Singh. (See also pages 26–27.)

Flag-changing
Outside every gurdwara there is a flagpole where the Sikh flag, the Nishan Sahib, flies all year round. The flagpole is covered with a saffron-yellow cloth which is changed at Baisakhi. (See also pages 28–31.)

I care about equal opportunities, that's racially and between the sexes. Equal opportunity is what Sikhs believe in. Whether you're a man or a woman, you're equal as a Sikh.

There are certain groups in society that are racist. Sikhs are totally against that type of thing. Nearly every Indian has had to cope with some sort of racial harassment. There are rallies against racism. I've been to a few of those.

BACHITTAR SINGH

MY FAVOURITE FESTIVAL

As a Sikh, I would have to say that the most important festival is Baisakhi, the Birthday of the Khalsa, when the first Sikhs were initiated by our tenth and last Guru, Guru Gobind Singh. But the one I prefer is Basant Panchami, which is a very popular festival in India.

Basant Panchami is celebrated during February/March, when the spring season starts and the days begin getting warmer. This change in the weather seems to trigger a mood of happiness, freedom and togetherness in everyone. It's also the time when the mustard crop is brought in. Wherever you go, the fields look yellow with the bloom of crops. People gather in open places, men with yellow turbans, women with yellow scarves, children with yellow dresses – in honour of the commencement of the spring season. They have a lot of fun.

At that festival, there are funfairs, people sing a lot of songs, songs like 'Basant Ayee' ('The Weather is Changing'), and everywhere you look people are happy. The sky is full of colourful kites. Yes, kite-flying is the most popular game of the day – small kites, fancy kites flown all around. Skilful flyers use starched strings and fight a less-skilled opponent. One string grinds through the other and the loser's kite starts dropping. The excitement of the day is beyond what words can explain.

Sikhs, Hindus, Muslims, Christians – everyone participates. There's a great sense of unity, the sort of unity we need more of with the world in its present state. Sikhs also go to the gurdwaras. There are hymns in the Guru Granth Sahib about the Basant festival. But what I like most is the way that, in India, it brings the religions together. I like it because it creates unity.

PARTAP SINGH

FACT-FINDER

Khalsa • Guru Gobind Singh
The Khalsa is the organization or fellowship of pure Sikhs. Ranjit describes what happened on the first Baisakhi on pages 26–27.

Guru Granth Sahib
The Sikhs' sacred scriptures.

MY FAVOURITE FESTIVAL

My particular favourite festival is Baisakhi. There's a lot of pomp and ceremony, lots of action. The mood, the atmosphere, at that time is really nice. I enjoy April coming up every year because it's sort of like Christmas for Christians. It's something you really look forward to. Also, it's the Sikh festival which is celebrated the most in this country.

Loads and loads of things go on, not just in Sikh temples but in the Sikh community as well. You have street processions in April. You have many well-known people coming to Sikh temples and performing religious hymns or giving religious sermons which are interesting to go and listen to. You have the annual baptizing ceremony taking place for those who want to be baptized. There are a lot of events for children, too. They have camps and things like that where they can go and be with their own age-group. They learn about the religion as well as having fun and games.

PRITPAL SINGH B

FACT-FINDER

Baisakhi
Festival on 13 April celebrating the founding of the Khalsa, the organization or fellowship of pure Sikhs, by Guru Gobind Singh. (See also pages 26–27.)

Baptizing ceremony
The Amrit ceremony at which Sikhs are initiated into (become members of) the Khalsa (see above). Amrit is sacred sugared water.

MY FAVOURITE FESTIVAL

Guru Nanak was the founder of the Sikh religion, and the first festival Sikhs celebrate is Guru Nanak's Birthday. They do this all over the world with great pomp and show. Like Easter, its date changes with the lunar calendar, but usually it's in November. The date of the second important festival stays the same every year at April 13th. This is Baisakhi.

Baisakhi is the day on which the Khalsa was born. It happened on 13th April 1699 when Guru Gobind Singh, the tenth and last Guru, called a big meeting of his followers in a hilly place called Anandpur.

Guru Gobind Singh preached the same principles as Guru Nanak, but he gave them their finishing touches. This was a time of Mughal rule in India. There was religious oppression. Indian people, most of them Hindus, were being forced to convert to Islam. Guru Gobind Singh said it was time for people to stand up for their freedom. For instance, the Mughal rulers said you couldn't ride a horse. Guru Gobind Singh encouraged his followers to ride a horse. The Mughal rulers said you couldn't build a platform more than five feet high – this was the height of the Mughal throne in Delhi. The Sixth Guru, Guru Har Gobind, had raised a platform seven feet high in Amritsar. These were the gestures of freedom fighters. Guru Gobind Singh said, 'Any person who will be brave and bold, let him be a Sikh.' And at Anandpur he put the Sikhs to the test.

He stood at the front of a big meeting of the Sikhs with his sword in his hand. He said he wanted true followers who were prepared to offer their heads. People were surprised. He'd never asked for anything like this before. One person stepped forward and offered himself. He was Daya Ram. 'Daya' means 'merciful'; a Sikh must be merciful. The Guru took him away.

With his sword dripping with blood, the Guru returned to the meeting. People were frightened and embarrassed. They started drifting away. What had happened to the Guru? Then Dharam Das offered his head. 'Dharam' means 'dutiful'; a Sikh must be true to his duties. In the same way, he also offered his head as a sacrifice for his Guru.

Three more Sikhs came forward. They were Himmat Rai, Mukham Chand and Sahib Chand. 'Himmat' is courage; 'Mukham' means submission, and we must submit ourselves to our God or to our guru or to our prophet. Each of these three was led into a tent as before, and each time the Guru returned with his sword dripping with blood.

FACT-FINDER

Lunar calendar
Calendar in which a new month starts when there is a new moon, i.e. every twenty-nine or thirty days.

Anandpur • Amritsar
Both of these places are in the Punjab in north-west India. Amritsar is where the Fifth Guru had built the Golden Temple, the most sacred place for Sikhs.

Mughal rule
The Muslim Mughals (or Moguls) controlled much of northern India between 1526 and 1857. Some of the Mughal emperors treated their Sikh and Hindu subjects well, others did not.

Sixth Guru, Har Gobind (1595–1645)
Often called the Warrior Guru because he was the military as well as the spiritual leader of the Sikhs. When he became Guru, Har Gobind said that instead of prayer-beads he would wear two swords. One would be a symbol of spiritual power, the other of worldly power. The platform at Amritsar which he built is called the Akal Takht (see also page 34).

Singhs
As well as baptizing the Panj Piare, the Guru gave them all the name Singh, meaning 'lion'. He said that all male members of the Khalsa (including himself) should share this name. All female members should take the name Kaur, meaning 'princess'.

This was the way the Guru chose his Five Beloved Ones, the Panj Piare. When a Sikh has the five qualities of the Five Beloved Ones, he becomes a sahib, a master, an equal. Having chosen the Panj Piare, Guru Gobind Singh restored their heads. Sikhs believe that the Guru is able to do anything.

To the Five Beloved Ones, Guru Gobind Singh said, 'I know I am with you and you are with me.' He was in effect decreeing that there would be no human Gurus after him. He was creating a sort of democracy: Singhs who would gather together and take collective decisions for the future well being of the Sikh religion when there was no longer a human Guru to guide them. Later he was to ask the Sikhs to accept the teachings of the Gurus – collected in the Guru Granth Sahib – as our next Guru. He said there was no more need of a human Guru. Men die but their words live on. Indeed, the words in the Guru Granth Sahib are the words of the Gurus – their compositions, written by them in their own lifetime. We have no authority to change a single word of what they wrote.

Guru Gobind Singh then baptized the Five Beloved Ones. He took a steel bowl and into it he put fresh water and some sugar cakes we call patashas. Then he took a khanda, a double-edged sword, and started stirring, singing a hymn to each of the Five Beloved Ones in turn. Those hymns are contained in the Guru Granth Sahib. Some are long, some short, and they take about an hour to perform. As he added the patashas, the Guru said, 'Just as I am mixing sugar into water to make Amrit ['amrit' means nectar], so should this Khalsa we are creating be sweet, not cruel.' When the Amrit was prepared, he put a drop into the ears, eyes and mouths of each of the Five Beloved Ones, saying, 'I have created a pure Khalsa. These men will be pure. This Khalsa belongs to God. God's name is victory.'

Then the Guru bowed before the Five Beloved Ones saying, 'I have not yet been baptized. I now bow before you. You must baptize me.' So the Five Beloved Ones baptized the Guru in the same way he had baptized them. That's why we say, 'Wahuwah, Gobind Singh. Apé Gur chela.' That is, 'Gobind Singh is wonderful. He's a Guru and a disciple, too.' First he was Guru, then he created disciples, then by his disciples he was made a disciple.

From that first baptism followed others. Many Sikhs were baptized that day in April 1699. Countless Sikhs have been baptized into the Khalsa since then. So that day was the beginning of Sikhism as an organization. We call it the Birth of the Khalsa.

RANJIT SINGH

MY FAVOURITE FESTIVAL

At Baisakhi, because secondary schools here are predominantly Asian, I go round to some of them and tell the Baisakhi story. I do a very simple story of Baisakhi which lasts for about thirty-five minutes and tells what happened to Guru Gobind Singh and how Sikhism came about.

I think Baisakhi has so much to offer in a school situation. Of course, it has to be tackled sensitively. A lot of Sikh history is tied up with a particular phase of Muslim history in northern India – Aurangzeb and what happened then, for instance. The story-telling approach is good, though. It provides something you could never get out of a book – experience and emotion and feelings. Partly, I suppose, because I'm celebrating something which is so important to me.

My son and daughter were in a different gurdwara from me on Baisakhi day this year. Tejpal, the four-year-old, told me all about how they took the flag down and washed the pole. Next year, he'll see a bit more, ask more questions, understand a bit more. Rupi, our younger child, enjoyed the running around, but she picked up on the flag coming down. These are important starting-points. As they get older, bit by bit they'll start piecing together the whole story. It's their inheritance.

RAMINDER SINGH V

FACT-FINDER

Baisakhi
Ranjit describes what happened on the first Baisakhi, in 1699, on pages 26–27.

Muslim history ... Aurangzeb • Mughal empire
The Muslim Mughals (or Moguls) controlled much of northern India between 1526 and 1857. Some of the Mughal emperors treated their Sikh and Hindu subjects well. However, the strongly pro-Islamic policies of Jehangir (ruled 1628–1658) and Aurangzeb (ruled 1658–1707) led to conflict with the Sikhs.

Took the flag down
Outside every gurdwara there is a flagpole where the Sikh flag, the Nishan Sahib, flies all year round. The flagpole is covered with a saffron-yellow cloth which is changed at Baisakhi. The pole is lowered, washed with yoghurt or milk and rinsed with water before the new covering is put on.

Khalsa • Panj Piare • Guru Gobind Singh
'Panj Piare', meaning 'Five Beloved Ones', is the name given by Guru Gobind Singh to the five men who volunteered to die for their faith on the first Baisakhi. The five were baptized by the Guru with Amrit (sacred sugared water) and became the first members of the Khalsa, the organization or fellowship of pure Sikhs. (See also pages 26–27.)

Baisakhi's my favourite festival. That's the day when the Khalsa was born, when the Sikh religion was born, when the Panj Piare became Sikhs. It's when the religion started.

Guru Gobind Singh felt that people should stick up for their rights. This was at the time of the Mughal empire, when people – Hindu people, mainly – were being converted by force to Islam. Guru Gobind Singh stood up against that sort of oppression, and that's another reason why the festival is important to me.

BACHITTAR SINGH

MY FAVOURITE FESTIVAL

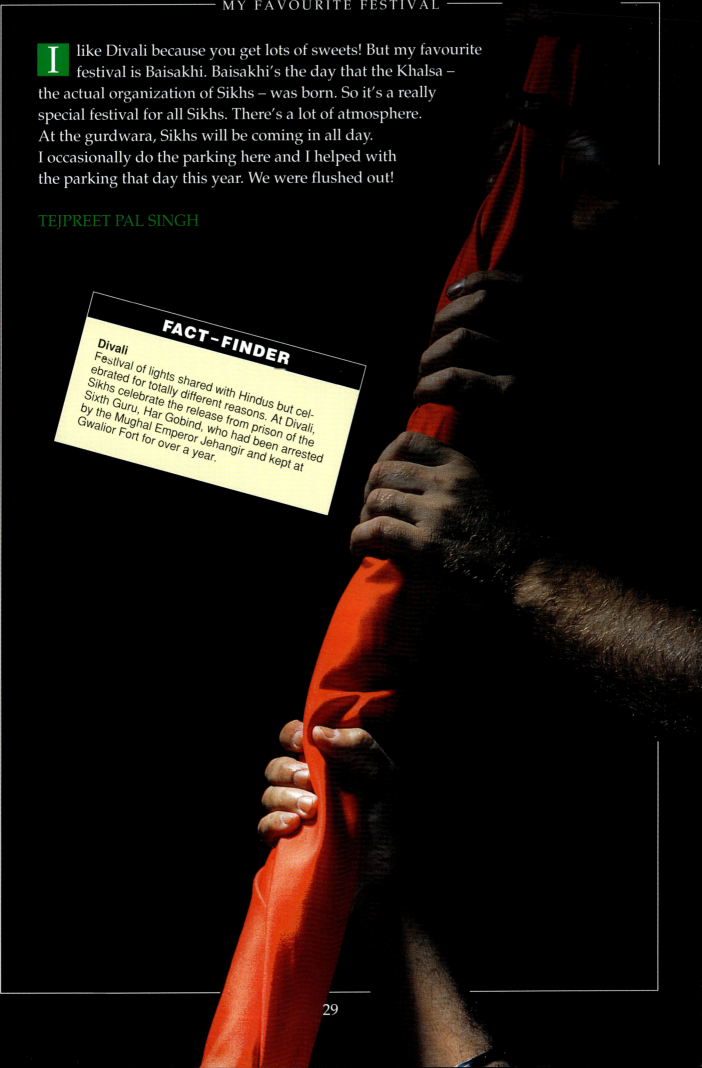

I like Divali because you get lots of sweets! But my favourite festival is Baisakhi. Baisakhi's the day that the Khalsa – the actual organization of Sikhs – was born. So it's a really special festival for all Sikhs. There's a lot of atmosphere. At the gurdwara, Sikhs will be coming in all day. I occasionally do the parking here and I helped with the parking that day this year. We were flushed out!

TEJPREET PAL SINGH

FACT-FINDER

Divali
Festival of lights shared with Hindus but celebrated for totally different reasons. At Divali, Sikhs celebrate the release from prison of the Sixth Guru, Har Gobind, who had been arrested by the Mughal Emperor Jehangir and kept at Gwalior Fort for over a year.

MY FAVOURITE FESTIVAL

I like the end-of-the-year celebration here – the end of the calendar year, not the Sikh year. It's not exactly a festival. We come to the temple at night. Everyone's around. There are loads of kirtan.

I like Baisakhi, too. In the temple in the morning, first the Panj Piare process in. Then we do the Ardas. After that, the Panj Piare go out and change the flag. I don't know exactly what happens at that point because there are loads of people around and it's difficult to see! Everyone has their own way of changing the flag depending on where the flag is. In Southall, it used to be on the roof, and the Panj Piare took it down and put milk on the pole. Here it's on a flagpole at ground level and everybody gets involved in changing it.

What I like about Baisakhi is that everybody gets together. You're with people you have a lot in common with.

MANJIT KAUR B

FACT-FINDER

Kirtan
Singing hymns (sacred songs) from the Guru Granth Sahib, the Sikhs' sacred scriptures.

Baisakhi
Baisakhi celebrates the founding of the Khalsa, the organization or fellowship of pure Sikhs, by Guru Gobind Singh.

Panj Piare
Here, five Sikhs representing the original Panj Piare (see opposite).

Ardas
Literally, 'prayer'. Name used for the prayer said by the congregation at the end of most Sikh religious ceremonies.

Changing the flag
Outside every gurdwara there is a flagpole where the Sikh flag, the Nishan Sahib, flies all year round. The flagpole is covered with a saffron-yellow cloth which is changed at Baisakhi. The pole is washed with yoghurt or milk and rinsed with water before the new covering is put on.

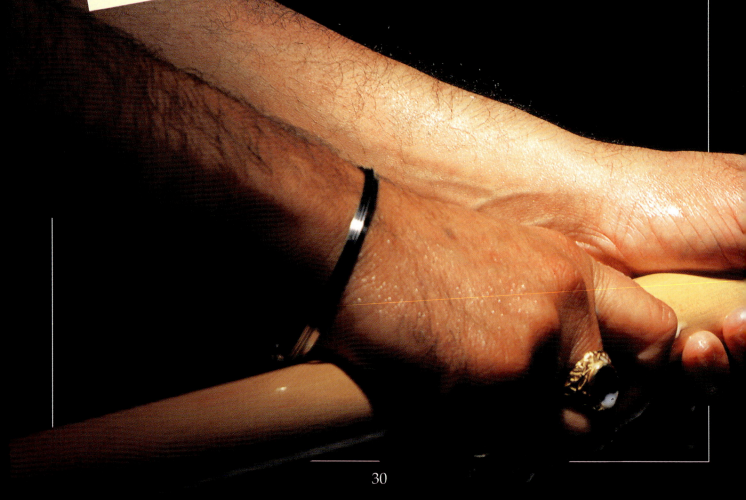

MY FAVOURITE FESTIVAL

Every year, Baisakhi just moves me to bits. The moment of the flag-changing and the significance we give it, that's such an important focus. The whole community turns up.

This is the day on which the original Panj Piare (the Five Beloved Ones) were chosen, and at Baisakhi we have the Panj Piare leading the ceremony. They're in their uniforms, with their beards opened and wearing full turbans and everything. I think, 'That's *our* uniform.' The whole day, the preaching and everything that follows, is special to me. We're celebrating the day when Sikhism actually came into being, when we found our identity.

ANEET KAUR V

FACT-FINDER

Flag-changing
See opposite.

Panj Piare
Name originally given by Guru Gobind Singh to the five men who volunteered to sacrifice themselves for their faith on the first Baisakhi. The five were baptized by the Guru with Amrit (sacred sugared water) and became the first members of the Khalsa, the organization or fellowship of pure Sikhs. (See also pages 26–27.)

The name Panj Piare is also given to the five respected members of a Sikh community who conduct the Amrit ceremony and carry the Nishan Sahib in religious processions. Their uniforms are a yellow robe with a blue sash (see page 12).

With their beards opened
With their beards combed out to their full length, i.e. not confined in a beard net. Sikhs sometimes use a net to keep their beard tidy.

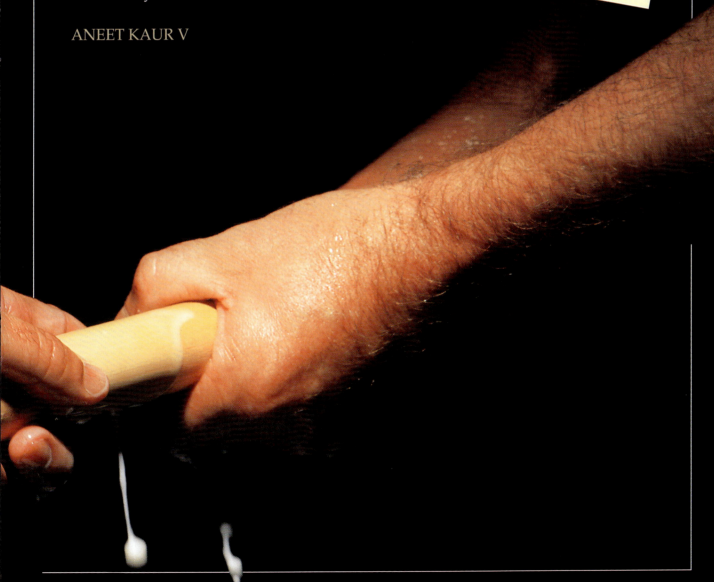

A SPECIAL MOMENT

I think marriage is a special moment. Our marriage was a special moment for me, and I'm reminded of it when I go to other people's weddings.

Yesterday, Aneet and I went to the church wedding of a friend of ours. The bride wore a beautiful white gown and the groom was there with top hat and morning suit. It was great. Afterwards Aneet and I were talking about it. Father Lawrence, the priest, had referred to a wedding of two families, and that's how marriage had been described at our wedding, too. It's a marriage of two individuals, but it's also the bringing together of two families. The words used at a Sikh wedding talk about the marriage of two families, two cultures, two bodies.

That's why marriage has so much significance. I didn't know Aneet well when we got married. Our marriage was arranged to the extent that we had the final say, and we did go out very discreetly beforehand. But it was the marriage of two families to start with, and we built our love on that rather than the love coming first.

To me, marriage is so important that you *have* to work at it. It's not given to you on a plate. Working at marriage is part of the values and attitudes that get passed on to you in a Sikh family from a very young age. There are attitudes towards children growing up, attitudes towards respect for other people. They all seem to come together in the marriage package. So it wasn't daunting in any way that we were married without knowing that much about each other, because we knew what would be ahead of us. We brought to our marriage values and attitudes that both of us were familiar with.

So the special moment of my life was marriage, going around the Guru Granth Sahib.

RAMINDER SINGH V

FACT-FINDER

Values
Ideas about what is right, what is wrong, what is of real value in life and how people should behave.

Going around the Guru Granth Sahib
At a Sikh wedding, the groom leads his bride four times around the Guru Granth Sahib, the Sikhs' sacred scriptures. This is the most important part of the marriage ceremony.

A SPECIAL MOMENT

In our family, we have the Guru Granth Sahib brought to our home every Christmas for a ceremony called Akhand Path. It lasts for three days, and during that time the whole of Guru Granth Sahib is read. That's a special time to me. A lot of people get invited to the house. You see everybody you know.

The Guru Granth Sahib comes from the temple. If you want it, you can ask for it and it comes to your home. Our family does the Akhand Path at Christmas because that's our tradition. Others might do it when they've bought a new house or something like that, to bring good luck.

Anybody can read from the Guru Granth Sahib. There isn't anything to stop me, for instance – except that it's very difficult. My uncle can read it. So can my cousin.

MANJIT KAUR B

> **FACT-FINDER**
>
> **Guru Granth Sahib**
> The Sikhs' sacred scriptures.
>
> **Akhand Path**
> Uninterrupted reading of the Guru Granth Sahib from beginning to end by a team of readers. The words must be read clearly so that people listening can understand them. At the end of the reading, which usually lasts about forty-eight hours, a formal ceremony called a 'bhog' completes the Akhand Path. This involves saying the Ardas (see page 30), taking a hukam (reading selected at random from the Guru Granth Sahib and respected as God's command by the Sikhs present) and sharing karah parshad (sweet food eaten at each Sikh ceremony).

A SPECIAL MOMENT

Have you heard about the Akal Takht? 'Akal' means God, 'takht' is a throne. The Akal Takht is in Amritsar. It's a platform seven feet high which the Sixth Guru built. Any order issued from that place has to be obeyed by Sikhs.

I was a lad of twelve, living in the Punjab and still at school. The schoolchildren were asked whether any of us wanted to get baptized. I was one of those who offered themselves. The Five Beloved Ones came from Amritsar, from the Akal Takht, to initiate us. That was a special moment for me, a very important event in my life.

I got baptized when I was still quite young. I had my hair uncut though, even then, because hair is important to my family. And I was very happy and honoured to wear the Five K's.

Every initiated Sikh has to wear the Five K's. K is for 'kesh'. That's hair. Guru Gobind Singh said hair is a blessing from nature and that the Khalsa should be recognized by its uncut hair. I'm initiated and my hair is uncut. I can't deny that I'm a Sikh.

FACT-FINDER

Amritsar
City in the Punjab in north-west India where the Fifth Guru built the Golden Temple, the most sacred place for Sikhs.

Sixth Guru, Har Gobind (1595–1645)
See page 26.

Baptized • Initiated • Khalsa
Sikhs are baptized or initiated into (i.e. become members of) the Khalsa, the organization or fellowship of pure Sikhs, at a ceremony using Amrit (sacred sugared water).

Five Beloved Ones
Here, five Sikhs representing the original Five Beloved Ones (Panj Piare), the five men baptized by Guru Gobind Singh as the first five members of the Khalsa. (See also pages 26–27.)

A SPECIAL MOMENT

K is for 'kara', a steel band worn on the right wrist. This is a symbol of restraint. Before doing anything, you must ask yourself whether it is the right thing.

K is for 'kangha'. A kangha is a comb. Every morning a Sikh must comb his hair. I always carry a small comb under my turban.

K is for 'kirpan', a sword. This was a weapon to use in defence of your religious principles and to help other people needing protection. I carry a small sword.

K is for 'kachha'. This is special long underwear made to be comfortable, and worn for modesty.

RANJIT SINGH

When I went to Amritsar, that was special. I've only been to India a few times. When I first went I was very young, so I can't actually remember anything. A few years back now, we went again. I went to Amritsar and I can't find the words to describe how it felt. It was such a holy place. Everyone was praying. It was a wonderful feeling being there.

BACHITTAR SINGH

A SPECIAL MOMENT

I was initiated at Baisakhi this year. That has to be my personal special moment. It's the whole initiation ceremony that's special.

It's a personal moment because only the ones who are taking Amrit can be present at the ceremony with the Panj Piare. I'm not allowed to tell anyone about the ceremony, either. But I can say that it feels like a transformation. Before, it's like you're ninety-nine per cent Sikh, but you're not a proper Sikh. That ceremony transforms you. I suppose I can describe it like this: I've been born on earth, but when I took the actual sacred water it was like being born in the house of God, up in heaven.

TEJPREET PAL SINGH

FACT-FINDER

Baisakhi
Festival celebrating the founding of the Khalsa, the organization or fellowship of pure Sikhs, by Guru Gobind Singh. (See also pages 26–27.)

Initiated
Became a member of the Khalsa (see above).

Amrit
Sacred sugared water.

Panj Piare
Here, five respected members of the Sikh community who conduct the Amrit ceremony. (See also page 31.)

Mool Mantra
Sikhs regard this as the most important verse composed by Guru Nanak, the First Guru. The Mool Mantra sums up the Sikh idea of God but is difficult to translate because its wording is very concise. (See also page 38.)

It was last Baisakhi day. I was in the gurdwara with the children. Tejpal had just learnt the Mool Mantra. He turned to me and said, 'Mummy, everyone's going up on the stage and talking. I want to say something, too.'

Initially, I thought, 'No, there are too many people, he'll be scared.' I said this to Tejpal but he was quite certain: 'No, I won't be scared. I want to do it.' So I thought, 'Well, if that's what he wants, why not?' I said to him, 'What about saying the Mool Mantra. You know that very well.' He said, 'Yes, I'd like to do that.'

There was a congregation of about two hundred people. Tejpal stood up. I asked the person in charge, 'Do you think he could? He's only four-and-a-half.' Yes, he could. So Tejpal he went up on the stage, sat down and very clearly and loudly recited the Mool Mantra. It was so touching. That was a special moment.

ANEET KAUR V

I'm not sure about a special moment. I regard my whole life as being special. I'm grateful to God for giving me my life and I in turn thank God through the loyalty I have for him – or her. For the life I have I can only thank God, nobody else.

PRITPAL SINGH B

A SPECIAL MOMENT

In India, Hindu people celebrate a festival every year called Dussehra when they burn an effigy of the evil King Ravana. When I was about twelve and at school, I went with a group of my friends to see the festival.

There was a very big effigy of King Ravana. Its body section was stuffed with fireworks. When the fire eventually reached them, these fireworks shot high up into the sky. At first, my eyes were very pleased with all of this. Then I noticed that one firework was coming straight towards me. I started running this way and that. Whichever direction I turned, the firework followed me. I ran out of the crowd and onto the roadside. It hit my right leg. It was no longer burning, but it was still hot.

This was something that was going to happen to me, and I couldn't escape it. We Sikhs believe that what happens in our lives was written before our birth. It's our destiny. So I knew this was going to happen. And it did. I can never forget this special moment of my life.

PARTAP SINGH

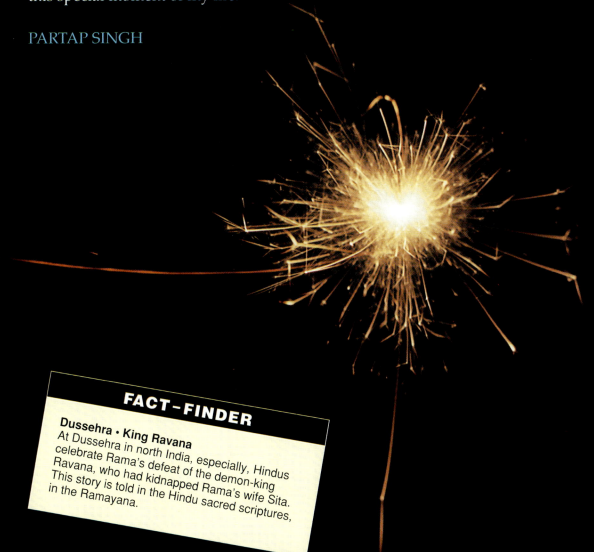

FACT-FINDER

Dussehra • King Ravana
At Dussehra in north India, especially, Hindus celebrate Rama's defeat of the demon-king Ravana, who had kidnapped Rama's wife Sita. This story is told in the Hindu sacred scriptures, in the Ramayana.

WORDS THAT MEAN A LOT TO ME

The very special words for me are right at the beginning of the Guru Granth Sahib. These are the Mool Mantra, Guru Nanak's Message:

Ik onkar ...	There is one God	੧ਓ
sat nam ...	his name is truth	ਸਤਿ ਨਾਮੁ
karta purkh ...	he is the creator	ਕਰਤਾ ਪੁਰਖ
nir bhau ...	without fear	ਨਿਰ ਭਉ
nir vair ...	without enemies	ਨਿਰ ਵੈਰੁ
akal murat ...	God beyond time	ਅਕਾਲ ਮੂਰਤਿ
arjuni ...	beyond birth and death	ਅਜੂਨੀ ਸੈਭੰ
sebhan ...	self-existent	ਗੁਰ ਪ੍ਰਸਾਦਿ ॥
Gurparsad ...	known by the grace of the Guru	

God is everywhere and we can get close to him through the grace of the Guru. So the Guru – the Guru Granth Sahib – is a very important factor in our lives. I think 'Guru' is the single most important word for me.

RANJIT SINGH

FACT-FINDER

Guru Granth Sahib
The Sikhs' sacred scriptures.

Mool Mantra
Sikhs regard this as the most important verse composed by Guru Nanak, the First Guru. The Mool Mantra sums up the Sikh idea of God but is difficult to translate because its wording is very concise. It is repeated in full or in an abbreviated version at the beginning of each section of the Guru Granth Sahib.

The grace of the Guru
The mercy, kindness or favour of the Guru, i.e. the Guru's help.

WORDS THAT MEAN A LOT TO ME

The words that mean most to me are in the Guru Granth Sahib just before the Japji Sahib. They're the most important words in the Guru Granth Sahib and they're called the Mool Mantra. You learn the Mool Mantra when you're a child. It explains what God is. I say it in the morning.

There are certain prayers you do at certain times. You say the Japji Sahib in the morning, after you've washed and everything. You're meant to wash every morning. Then you do your prayers, saying them to yourself.

If you can't say all of the Japji Sahib or any of the other daily prayers, you say the Mool Mantra instead.

MANJIT KAUR B

FACT-FINDER

Guru Granth Sahib
The Sikhs' sacred scriptures.

Japji Sahib • Mool Mantra
'Jap' means 'meditation', '-ji' and 'Sahib' are terms of respect meaning 'great' and 'master'. The Japji is one of the most important poems composed by Guru Nanak, the First Guru, and is the first hymn in the Guru Granth Sahib. Strictly speaking, the Mool Mantra (see opposite) is part of the Japji. Sikhs should meditate on the Japji every morning.

I think 'Ik onkar' – 'There is only one God' – is quite important. Sikhs believe that there is only one God. When we pray, we're reminded of that all the time. A lot of prayers start with 'Ik onkar'. 'Ik onkar' is right at the beginning of the Mool Mantra, which is right at the beginning of the Guru Granth Sahib. It's also at the start of the Japji Sahib, which I say every morning. I know about three-quarters of the Japji Sahib now.

BACHITTAR SINGH

WORDS THAT MEAN A LOT TO ME

I f I'm not feeling too good, I usually go and start reading the holy scriptures from the sentia. That gives me a wonderful sort of feeling. It makes me feel better and supports me. It seems amazing. I just have to sit down and pray for an hour and read the holy scriptures and I'll feel a lot better.

At the end of every service in the gurdwara, and when you read the holy scriptures at home, you just open the holy book at random and read from the first verse on the page. You're supposed to read from the holy scriptures in the morning and think for the rest of the day about what the Gurus have said in that verse. So if at any point you think of doing something bad, you also have the words of the Gurus going round in your mind, encouraging you to strive for something better.

> **FACT-FINDER**
>
> **Holy scriptures • Sentia**
> The Sikh holy scriptures are collected together in the Guru Granth Sahib, a large book with 1430 pages. Sentia are smaller books containing either the first or the second half of the Guru Granth Sahib and used for study and/or private reading.

PRITPAL SINGH B

T here's words and there's guidance. If I wanted guidance, I would probably turn to the Guru Granth Sahib. It's been written by the Gurus, so it guides us in our way of life. But I don't really have any special words. Words are important, but on their own I wouldn't turn to them for advice because they're just words.

Pictures can be special, and so can places. Pictures of the Gurus on the wall are special because they're pictures of God. We can't disrespect them. Even when we sleep, we can't put our feet towards them. I've got a picture of Guru Gobind Singh at home. It's to the side of my bed so that my feet don't face towards it.

Special places are gurdwaras, especially gurdwaras in the Punjab. There are gurdwaras in Pakistan, for instance, where there are special things like the stones and weaponry that our Gurus used to use. They've been touched by the Gurus. I haven't seen them yet, but I will go and see them because they're that special. I have to go and see them.

> **FACT-FINDER**
>
> **Guru Granth Sahib**
> The Sikhs' sacred scriptures.
>
> **Punjab**
> This region of north-west India where the Sikh religion began was split when India became independent of British rule in 1947. Almost three-quarters of the Punjab is now part of (Muslim) Pakistan. The remainder became the modern Indian state of Punjab.

TEJPREET PAL SINGH

WORDS THAT MEAN A LOT TO ME

For me, 'Waheguru' is very important. I find that if I'm worried about anything, that phrase comes naturally to me, any time of the day. I'm not required to say it or anything. What I was told as a child is that, even if you're talking or working, you should always be saying 'Waheguru' to yourself. If you do that, there's no chance of evil thoughts coming into your mind.

I find my little girl saying 'Waheguru' quite clearly now. She realizes that we all say 'Waheguru'. Going to bed, we say 'Waheguru'. Just before meals, we'll either say 'Waheguru' or we might say a short grace, like 'God, thank you for giving us this meal.' But our daughter has just picked up 'Waheguru' and she'll say it whenever we do.

ANEET KAUR V

FACT-FINDER

Waheguru
This means 'Wonderful Lord', a Sikh name for God.

WORDS THAT MEAN A LOT TO ME

Words are important. 'Waheguru' is important. So is the Mool Mantra. My son is now able to say the Mool Mantra quite easily. Aneet has taught him. And both my son and my daughter can say 'Waheguru'.

There are other words that go straight to the heart of my Sikh identity. For instance, there's the shout 'Bohe so nihal' and its reply 'Sat sri akal', which are said so passionately, especially at Baisakhi time.

Then there's the shabad De-shiva-Bar-mohe. When I was young my parents had a religious video. There is a scene in this video which shows a Sikh army marching, and getting ready for war. While they are marching, they are singing the shabad called De-shiva-Bar-mohe. This is sung so passionately that it made me feel so proud to be a Sikh. I mean, yes, you get your attitudes and values from your parents, but seeing that scene of the Sikh army singing, 'Raj karega Khalsa!' – it was tremendous. That was a moment when I could say, 'I belong to the Sikhs.'

RAMINDER SINGH V

FACT-FINDER

Waheguru
This means 'Wonderful Lord', a Sikh name for God.

Mool Mantra
See page 38.

Bohe so nihal
Often said in honour of someone, this means 'Let everyone who agrees say'.

Sat sri akal
Universal Sikh greeting, meaning 'Truth [God] is eternal'.

Baisakhi
Festival celebrating the founding of the Khalsa (see below) by Guru Gobind Singh. (See also pages 26–27.)

Shabad
The Word of God, often (as here) a hymn (sacred song) from the Guru Granth Sahib, the Sikh scriptures. The shabad De-shiva-Bar-mohe is also sometimes called the Sikh National Anthem.

Raj karega Khalsa
This means 'The Khalsa [the organization or fellowship of pure Sikhs] will rule', and is part of the battle-cry of the Sikhs in the eighteenth century. A longer phrase taken from this battle-cry, meaning 'The Khalsa will rule, no foe can resist', is said at the end of the Ardas, the prayer that concludes most Sikh religious ceremonies.

WORDS THAT MEAN A LOT TO ME

habad is the Word of God, the word we follow as Sikhs. So any shabad is important to me, equally important.

Then there's 'Waheguru'. This is spoken or recited in praise of God. When I say 'Waheguru', I'm thanking God for giving me everything that I have in my life. My faith is contained in this word. I believe that salvation lies in praising God.

An important prayer is the Mool Mantra. This states the basic concept of God, which comes before anything else. The Mool Mantra starts the Guru Granth Sahib. It starts the gurbanis, the hymns, in the Guru Granth Sahib, even if it is just the opening lines – 'Ik onkar, sat nam' – that appear. There is always a reminder, either at the beginning or at the end of each hymn, of 'Gurparsad', the last line of the Mool Mantra, which means that we attain everything by God's grace.

I believe in God. You'll notice that I have prayer-beads – mala, we call them. There are one hundred and eight. Every time I recite the Mool Mantra, I count one bead.

My belief is that God is one. If you're born into a Sikh family, you're a Sikh. If you're born into a Hindu family, you're a Hindu. But whether you're Sikh, Hindu, Muslim, Christian, the path is the same. We're all trying to reach the same place, and we do that by the grace of God. That's what I believe. So we must spend time in praise and meditation. We must remember him who has created us.

PARTAP SINGH

FACT-FINDER

Waheguru
This means 'Wonderful Lord', a Sikh name for God.

Mool Mantra
See also page 38.

Guru Granth Sahib
The Sikhs' sacred scriptures.

God's grace
The mercy, kindness or favour of God, i.e. God's help.

THINGS I FIND CHALLENGING

I know I haven't reached this point yet, but I think I'll find it challenging deciding what to do about college or university when I leave school.

The problem is going to be the social life. I'll find it hard mixing. We're not supposed to drink alcohol in our religion. Other students are bound to go to parties. They'll have a drink.

I'll probably go to a college or university close enough to home for me to drive there every day and get back in the evening.

MANJIT KAUR B

THINGS I FIND CHALLENGING

Nothing in life is challenging to me. I accept my life very easily. I have a regular life. For instance, I pray in the morning. I prayed for two hours this morning. I got up at five, bathed, opened the Guru Granth Sahib and read from it. Then I prayed for two hours: one hour in bed, one hour sitting on the floor.

I'm quite happy with my life.

RANJIT SINGH

I have to work hard at reading and understanding the Guru Granth Sahib. That's a challenge. The Guru Granth Sahib's a composition of hymns. What happens is that we learn how to say it first. Because I live in England, I've got a better command of English than I have of Punjabi. So firstly I have to learn how to say the words and get the pronunciation right. I have to work very hard, exceptionally hard in relation to someone who lives in the Punjab, to get an understanding of the holy book. It's very difficult.

After that, I start learning how to interpret what the Gurus have written down and what's contained in the hymns. It's a long process. I mean, the reading's OK. That you can pick up and only improve on with practice. But the verses which the Gurus have written have so much depth to them. Interpreting them is hard for someone who hasn't got fluency in Punjabi and a grasp of all the subtleties of the language. In the Punjab, you would only start learning the meaning of the Guru Granth Sahib after getting a university degree. That shows how difficult it is. I can sort of get the gist of some things, but not a lot. Not a lot.

To help with this study, I go to classes in Slough three evenings a week: on Tuesdays, Wednesdays and Thursdays. I don't learn from the actual Guru Granth Sahib. What we have is a set of two smaller books called sentia. One has the first half of the Guru Granth Sahib in it, the other has the second half. That's what we learn from.

PRITPAL SINGH B

FACT-FINDER

Guru Granth Sahib • Punjabi
The Guru Granth Sahib, the Sikhs' sacred scriptures, is mainly in Punjabi, a language spoken by people from the Punjab in north-west India/south-east Pakistan. The written form of Punjabi is called Gurmukhi script.

THINGS I FIND CHALLENGING

It's challenging talking to teaching colleagues sometimes and getting them to realize that children have their own identity. We live in a multicultural society. Some areas are more multicultural than others. Some haven't had to face up to the issues. But in an area that has, you don't expect a teacher to turn to you and say, 'Why do I have to teach about other cultures? These kids have come to this country, haven't they?' That's happened to me.

It's tempting just to have a go at someone who says that. But you have to work through it. You have to help people change their attitudes. That's a challenge to me, to let people see both sides of the coin.

RAMINDER SINGH V

What I find challenging is bringing up my children in a multicultural society. I think the pressures are too great. If they're not taught the right values now, my children won't consider themselves Sikhs as they grow older. It's very important to me that they're proud to be Sikhs and that they remain Sikhs.

I come from North London. Where I grew up, at that time there were very few Asians and even fewer Sikhs. At school, I was the only Sikh. I'd get asked, 'Why have you got long hair?' – things like that. Even now, you find a lot of Sikh children saying, 'I want to cut my hair because all my friends have cut theirs.'

Some schools are now getting children talking about religious identity. They'll have special Baisakhi assemblies and things like that. I think it's important for children not to feel their individuality in a negative way. It's important to talk more about different faiths so at least children can begin to understand. A lot of problems are based simply on ignorance. Prejudice sets in later.

ANEET KAUR V

TURKISH FAMILY DIES IN GERMAN HOSTEL BLAZE

ATTACK ON SHOPKEEPER RACIALLY MOTIVATED

FACT-FINDER

Values
Ideas about what is right, what is wrong, what is of real value in life and how people should behave.

Baisakhi
Festival celebrating the founding of the Khalsa, the organization or fellowship of pure Sikhs, by Guru Gobind Singh. (See also pages 26–27.)

THINGS I FIND CHALLENGING

I don't like racism. I hate racism. We might be different colours, but we're all the same, we're all human.

Racism is what I find challenging in this world. At this time, in this place, people like me are the minority – at the moment. So you get people like the National Front, they come down and start swearing at you. You've got to fight against that. It's hard. They might come to your house, beat you up, but you've got to fight it.
That's a challenge.

They're trying to get us out of the country. We're trying to stay here. I consider this is my home. They say it's their country. It's not their country, it's a free country.

Nothing has happened to me so far, but the problem's a local one. It's in Isleworth, and that's close by.

TEJPREET PAL SINGH

When I see the sorts of things that are happening now – war, crime, rape, these sorts of things – I feel there is something very wrong. Youngsters, and not just Sikh youngsters, are abandoning their religion. Some people say this is the effect of Western influence. But people don't have to spoil their future, turn their backs on what their elders have done in the past, abandon what religion has taught us.

God is truth. Guru Nanak gave us five principles for honest and truthful living: kirt karna (earning an honest living), wand chhakana (sharing food with others, the needy), nam japana (meditation on God's Name), dan karna (charity, giving to the needy) and ishnan karna (cleanliness). I see my Sikh community moving completely away from these things. People do come to the temples. They do follow our holy Guru Granth Sahib. But they're not keeping the symbols, the Five K's.
That's very upsetting to me.

I do believe that one day, by the grace of God, evil will die and good triumph.

PARTAP SINGH

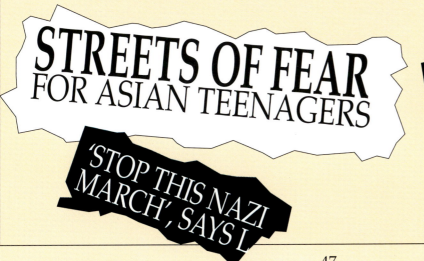

RACE BIAS JOBS ROW

STREETS OF FEAR FOR ASIAN TEENAGERS

'STOP THIS NAZI MARCH', SAYS L

FACT-FINDER

Guru Nanak (1469–1539)
The First Guru and founder of the Sikh faith.

Guru Granth Sahib
The Sikhs' sacred scriptures.

Five K's
The five symbols worn by Sikhs who are members of the Khalsa, the organization or fellowship of pure Sikhs. (See also pages 34–35.)

Grace of God
The mercy, kindness or favour of God, i.e. God's help.

INDEX

Page numbers in **bold** type show where words or phrases are explained in FACT-FINDERS

Akal Takht 26, 34
Akhand Path **33**
Alcohol 20, 21, 44
Amrit **21**, 27, **36**
  See also *Baptism*
Amritsar 26, **34**, 35
Anandpur 16, 26
Ardas **30**
Aurangzeb, Emperor **28**

Baisakhi **21**, **23**, 24, **25**, 26–27, 28, 29, 30, 31, **36**, **42**, 46
Baptism 16, **25**, 27, **34**, 36
Basant Panchami 24
Beards 20, 31
Bohe so nihal **42**

Caring for others 13, 14, 15, 18, 47
Community 10, 13, 17, 18, 19, 23, 30, 31, 42
Cultural tradition 10, 11, 17, 19, 32, 46

Divali 29
Dusshera 37

Equality 23, 47

Faith 18, 20, 21, 22, 23, 38, 43
Families 6, 10, 11, 12, 16, 17, 18, 21, 22, 23, 28, 32, 33, 34, 36, 41, 42, 43, 46
Five Beloved Ones See *Panj Piare*
Five K's **34**, 35, **47**
Flag-changing **23**, **28**, **30**, 31
Food 9, 13, 21, 47

Grace of God **43**, **47**
Gurbanis 43
  See also *Hymns*
Gurdwara activities/services 6, 7, 8, 9, 10, 13, 22, 24, 25, 28, 29, 30, 36, 40, 45
Gurmukhi 7, 45
Guru Arjan Dev **15**

Guru Gobind Singh 16, **24**, 26–27, **28**, 34, 40
Guru Granth Sahib 7, **24**, 27, 32, **33**, **38**, 39, **40**, **43**, **45**, 47
Guru Har Gobind 26, 34
Guru Nanak 16, 26, 38, 47

Hair 19, 21, 34–35, 46
  See also *Turbans*, *Beards*
Hymns 24, 25, 27, 43, 45
  See also *Kirtan*

Identity 10, 17, 18, 19, 20, 23, 31, 42, 46
Ik onkar 38, 39, 43
India 14, 16, 17, 18, 24, 26, 28, 34, 35, 37, 40, 45
Initiation 21, **34**, **36**
  See also *Baptism*

Japji Sahib 39

Kachha 35
Kangha 35
Kara 35
Kaur 26
Kesh 34
  See also *Hair*
Khalsa **21**, **24**, 26–27, **28**, 29, **34**, 42
Khanda 27
Kirpan 35
Kirtan **6**, **8**, **9**, 30

Langar 9, 13

Mala 43
Marriage 32
Meditation 43, 47
Mool Mantra **36**, **38**, 39, **42**, 43
Mother tongue See *Punjabi*
Mughals 26, **28**

Names 12, 13, 26
National Anthem 42
New Year 30
Nishan Sahib See *Flag-changing*

Panj Piare 26–27, **28**, 30, **31**, **34**, **36**
Praising God 43
Prayer 20, 35, 39, 40, 43, 45
Preaching 25, 31
Punjab 16, 26, **34**, 40, 45
Punjabi **6**, **45**
Punjabi school 6, **17**, **22**

Racism 23, 47
Raj karega Khalsa 42
Religious education 10, 19, 28

Sabha 4, 12
  See also *Community*
Sat sri akal **42**
Schools See *Punjabi school*, *Religious education*
Sewa **8**, 9
Shabad **42**, 43
Singh 12, **13**, **26**, 27
Singing See *Kirtan*
Smoking 21

Temple See *Gurdwara*
Thanking God 36, 41, 43
Time 11
Turbans 12, 20, 31

Values 17, 18, 19, **23**, 32, 42, **46**, 47

Waheguru **41**, **42**, **43**
Word of God See *Shabad*
Work 47
Worship 6, 7, 8, 9, 30

Young people 11, 17, 18, 19, 21, 23, 25, 28, 36, 44, 46, 47

48